The Prestige S

Associated Motorways

Keith Healey

© 2002 Keith Healey
ISBN 1 898432 57 0

Front cover: Typifying the Pool operation, and the Black & White fleet, in the 1960s, **8221 AD** was at Nottingham in September 1967. With "Associated Motorways" and "Cheltenham Spa" prominent in the destination screens there could have been no doubt as to its duties. *(G H F Atkins)*

Rear cover: The Associated Motorways house-style advertising - like that of so many other operators - included a stylised representation of a coach that bore little resemblance to the real thing. *(Keith Healey Collection)*

Title page: Greyhound **HU 4805**, an AEC 411 with Strachan & Brown 26-seat coachwork, is seen in Hammersmith a few weeks after its delivery in 1926. On the formation of the Pool in 1934 Greyhound was prepared to place all its express services therein, but the committee felt that the Bristol to London route did not fit in to the overall scheme. The service operated jointly with Royal Blue from 1933 to 1965. *(Tramway & Railway World)*

>> *Opposite page:* Seen in Nottingham towards the end of its active life, Black & White **DDF 49** was a 1939 Bristol L6G with Duple coachwork. The first year of operation into Nottingham by the company was 1929 and they always operated on the Cheltenham - Nottingham route. *(G H F Atkins)*

Below: Leyland Lion LT5 **TF 9100**, although in full Black & White livery, was a Leyland Motors demonstrator that never entered the fleet. In 1933 it passed to the Birmingham-based Gliderways, the trading name of H Morris. *(Senior Transport Archive/BCVM)*

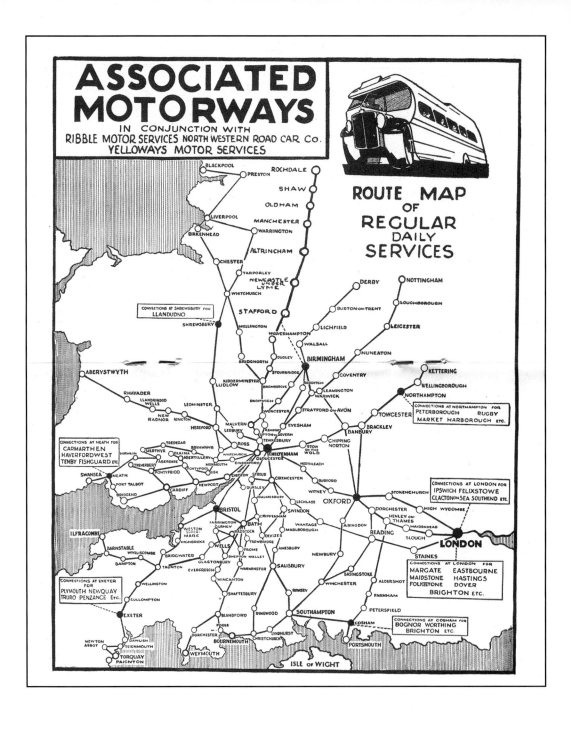

Above: The original 1934 route map was amended in 1937 with the hand-drawn addition of the Yelloway service northwards from Wolverhampton. This map was included in a special 40-page booklet offering inclusive holidays that included hotels and excursions and using Pool services. (Keith Healey Collection)

>> ***Opposite page:** There was very little of the country not accessible via Associated Motorways according to this map from the 1950s. (Keith Healey Collection)*

ASSOCIATED MOTORWAYS
ROUTE MAP
and Connecting Services

Sydenhams, Printers, Bournemouth

BLACK & WHITE MOTORWAYS Ltd.
RED & WHITE SERVICES Ltd.
BIRMINGHAM & MIDLAND MOTOR
OMNIBUS Co. Ltd.

WESTERN NATIONAL OMNIBUS Co. Ltd.
SOUTHERN NATIONAL OMNIBUS Co. Ltd.
BRISTOL TRAMWAYS & CARRIAGE Co. Ltd.
UNITED COUNTIES OMNIBUS Co. Ltd.

CENTRAL ORGANIZATION
MOTOR COACH STATION, CHELTENHAM
TEL. 3067

Acknowledgements

Much of the information for this book has been obtained from official records; acknowledgement has nonetheless to be made to three gentlemen who, over 50 years ago, replied to a young enthusiast's letters and took the time to explain what Associated Motorways was all about. They were Clem Preece (Royal Blue), William Combs (Secretary, Management Committee) and Ken Cope (Midland Red). Over the years I filed away everything written in the trade magazines about the "Pool" by those three and by H R Lapper of Black & White, and William Lambden of "Bus & Coach", who always enjoyed his visits to Cheltenham.

The excellent summaries of Traffic Court and Appeal Decisions written by Duncan and Michael Jewell together with Cobbett and Coachman in various trade publications refreshed my memory on points I had forgotten.

Thanks must also go to the Greater Manchester Transport Society and the National Tramway Society for allowing access to their archives; to Dave Haddock's Yelloway Museum for answering many of the questions that arose regarding that Company; to Geoffrey Atkins for some fine photographs; to Dave and Mary Shaw, and Roy Marshall, for reading the text in proof form, to its great benefit; and to Ron Maybray who has provided much detail of the individual vehicles illustrated.

To avoid confusion, from 1934 Associated Motorways will be referred to as the Pool, Western and Southern National as Royal Blue and Bristol Tramways as Greyhound throughout the text.

Keith Healey
Altrincham, Cheshire, June 2002

Introduction

This is the story of an organisation that owned no coaches but at a peak weekend could have over eight hundred vehicles on the road operating its services.

The formation of Associated Motorways has its roots in the 1920s when long distance travel was in its infancy. The various rail and coal strikes had brought home to the travelling public that there was an alternative to rail travel. More and more operators commenced long distance road services, principally to London from the provinces. By the end of the 1920s both bus and coach services had increased dramatically to such an extent that timetable booklets covering the whole of Britain were being published on the lines of the railway's Bradshaw; the first one, issued in 1929, ran to over a thousand pages.

To try and control all these services new legislation was brought in via the 1930 Road Traffic Act. The licensing of routes was taken out of the hands of local councils and placed with the newly formed Traffic Commissioners; Great Britain was, to begin with, divided into thirteen Traffic Areas. Each service had to have been in operation prior to February 1931 and registered with the appropriate Traffic Area by March 1931. This brought about a spate of new services in late 1930 so that they could be registered under the new Act. Herbert Morrison, the Minister of Transport, warned that these new services would have very little chance of being licensed if necessity could not be proven. Under the new Act various organisations were allowed to object to the grant of any licence, including operators with services on or near the proposed new route; this was liberally interpreted by some objectors, for example police and local councils on road safety; the biggest objector would be the main line railways - even though they had equal shareholdings in certain road operators. Their influence was great, and they managed to have imposed restrictions on duplication, periods of operation and fares, especially on long distance services.

By 1932 many small operators were struggling in a declining market. Quite a few were selling up, subject of course to the Traffic Commissioners granting a licence to the buyer. In many cases the Commissioners took the opportunity to reduce the services operated and at the same time various Chairmen were concerned by the number of services which duplicated each other, for example the route from Birmingham to Bournemouth was served by six different operators with the timings compressed between 8.15am and 10.40am. Suggestions were made that operators should meet and try to present a co-ordinated timetable for common routes, in default of which the Licensing Authorities might be forced to take action.

It was with this background that Red & White commenced talks with Black & White on the co-ordination of their London - South Wales services. Elliott Bros were also considering the same idea but on services between the Midlands and the South-West. So began a series of meetings lasting two years. The first was held at Cheltenham on 8th June 1932 among Elliott Bros, Black & White, Midland Red and Greyhound. This was followed by a further meeting, excluding Elliott Bros but including Ribble, to discuss the Elliott Bros scheme. It was now time to include the railway companies and obtain their thoughts on the proposals. The two independent operators, Elliott Bros and Red & White, were not invited to these talks. Meanwhile the co-ordination of the South Wales routes continued with the final grant of licences on 20th December 1933 from the Metropolitan Traffic Area.

By now, two pool schemes had been presented to the various operators concerned; one of them excluded Elliott Bros but this was not taken up and they were included in the final scheme. This meant that Red & White and Black & White would transfer all their express services to the Pool. Greyhound wanted to do the same but the London - Bristol route was not accepted. Midland Red, Elliott Bros and United Counties would transfer their Express Services from the Midlands to Bournemouth and Torquay only into the Pool as well as linking into Cheltenham from their respective areas.

A minor Pool was formed on 19th March 1934, consisting of Black & White, Red & White, Midland Red and Greyhound, for services between London to South Wales and the Midlands to Cheltenham and the South-West. This also included the London - Aberystwyth and Cardiff - Blackpool routes, neither of which called at Cheltenham. This Pool was replaced on 4th July by the Associated Motorways scheme centred at Cheltenham Coach Station and controlled by a Management Committee. To keep things tidy for financial reasons the Pool commenced on 1st July with the minor Pool ending on 30th June.

The Founder Members of Associated Motorways

Black & White Motorways, Cheltenham

In 1926 George Reading commenced a service between his hometown of Cheltenham and London. Over the years more destinations, including the Midlands, South Wales, Bournemouth and Torquay, were added. By 1930 the Company had been purchased jointly by Midland Red 40%, Bristol Tramways 40% and City of Oxford Motor Service 20%.

One year later a coach station had been built in St Margarets Road, Cheltenham, enabling the company to move from the Promenade. The interchange of passengers between services could now be achieved smoothly within the amenities of a modern coach station. It also served the citizens of the Spa as well with car parking and the use of the café and restaurants before or after a theatre or cinema visit.

The company continued to expand with the purchase of the Ensign Motor Coaches route between London and Aberystwyth in 1932; this was the first route not calling at Cheltenham. The following year the Link Safety Coaches Birmingham to Bournemouth route was purchased. The service was truncated at Oxford in agreement with Midland Red who paid part of the purchase price for the elimination of competition between Birmingham and Oxford. In the same year, jointly with Red & White, the London - Llanelly service of South Wales Express was taken over. Black & White were also considering the purchase of the Varsity Express Motors Oxford to London service but unless the South Midland route between the two cities was also purchased it would not have been economically viable.

Commencing on 1st July 1934 Black & White placed the following routes in the Pool:

London - Worcester - Aberystwyth
Cheltenham - London
Cheltenham - Cardiff - Swansea
Cheltenham - Leicester - Nottingham
Cheltenham - Bath - Bournemouth
Cheltenham - Hereford - Shrewsbury
Cheltenham - Birmingham -
                    Wolverhampton
Cheltenham - Burton upon Trent - Derby
Cheltenham - Southampton - Southsea
Cheltenham - Hereford - Aberystwyth
Cheltenham - Exeter - Paignton
Cheltenham - Northampton - Kettering
Cheltenham - Bristol - Weston super Mare
Cheltenham - Weston super Mare (Day
                    Excursion)

Percentage of Scheduled Mileage
38.428%
Percentage of Revenue 39.831%

Red & White Services, Chepstow

This company was formed through the amalgamation of a small group of operators in South Wales, which by 1929 were led by the pioneers John Watts and Guy Bown.

In that year long distance coach services were being operated by linking at Gloucester Coach Station with routes from South Wales, Birmingham, London, Plymouth and Bournemouth. The original London route was in conjunction with Rural England Motor Services; a disagreement between the two companies resulted in a new arrangement with Blue Star Coaches, in which Red & White took a financial interest.

The London - South Wales routes were

highly competitive: Black & White and Red & White ran alongside such concerns as Great Western Express, Cooks Safety Coaches, Fishers of Newport, South Wales Express, Cliffs Coaches and Queens Line. Additional services were operated between London and Gloucester by Red & Black (E Gray and Sons) and the Red Bus Service. The most unlikely operator was Westcliffe on Sea Motor Services, which, in 1929, commenced a thrice-daily London - Cardiff service under the name of "The Welsh Pullman". By the time the Road Traffic Act came into force many operators had dropped by the wayside and Red & White started to purchase those that had obtained Road Service Licences, commencing with Great Western Express in 1932; South Wales Express and Cliffs Coaches, which had combined their routes, were taken over in 1933 jointly with Black & White; Red Bus Service was acquired in the same year. Red & White were also looking further afield and made other financial investments including Nell Gwynne Coaches (Cardiff - Blackpool), Samuelsons (London - Liverpool), MacShanes (Liverpool - Torquay/ Glasgow/ London) and All British Travel (London - Liverpool/ North Wales). All these services will be referred to later.

In 1934 the following routes were placed in the Pool. Originally the routes shown as commencing from Cheltenham would have been from Gloucester, being changed when it was decided the interchange should be at Cheltenham after the co-ordination with Black & White in 1933:

Cardiff - Blackpool
Cheltenham - Oxford - London
Cheltenham - Reading - London
Gloucester - Reading - London
Cheltenham - Bath - Bournemouth
Cheltenham - Bristol - Paignton
Cheltenham - Worcester - Birmingham
Cheltenham - Cardiff - Swansea
Cheltenham - Tredegar - Swansea
Cheltenham - Pontypool - Blaina
Cheltenham - Aberdare - Treherbert
Cheltenham - Pontypridd - Treherbert
Cardiff - Mountain Ash - Aberdare

Percentage of Scheduled Mileage

Above: Greyhound Bristol B-type **HW 9506** is shown leaving Ilfracombe on the joint service to Liverpool a few days after its commencement in May 1931. By interchanging at Bristol with the Paignton - Liverpool service, also operated jointly with the Merseyside Touring Co, a further selection of destinations in the North-West were made available. *(G H F Atkins)*

Below: **RU 6728**, a 1928 ADC 424 with Duple 26-seat coachwork, was one of the eight ADCs transferred from Elliott Bros, after their purchase of the latter in 1935 by Thomas Tilling, to Hants & Dorset, along with the Bournemouth excursion licences. All eight vehicles were immediately sold. *(G H F Atkins)*

22.953%
Percentage of Revenue 22.953%

Elliott Bros (Bournemouth) Ltd t/a Royal Blue Automobile Services, Bournemouth

The company was registered in May 1921 although the family business can be traced back to 1880.

The first venture into express coach services was in 1919 with a service to London during the rail strike. This continued and by 1921 was operating twice daily. From 1928 routes were extended to link Birmingham and the Midlands with Bournemouth/Southsea and Plymouth picking up and setting down at all the towns en route.

In 1933 they purchased Traveller Saloon Coaches of Plymouth, which ran between that city and Portsmouth. Traveller Saloon had in the previous year purchased Olympic Motor Services of Portsmouth, which operated twice daily between Bristol and Southsea.

In the same year negotiations had taken place for the purchase of Highways Ltd, operating from London to North/South Devon and North Cornwall. The negotiations broke down and Highways was purchased by

Western and Southern National adding to the services to London already operated by these two companies. To avoid unnecessary competition pooling arrangements were entered into on certain routes by Western National and Royal Blue.

In July 1934 the following routes were placed in the Pool:

Bournemouth - Cheltenham - Coventry
Plymouth - Paignton - Worcester -
                    Birmingham
Bournemouth - Salisbury - Bristol
Bournemouth - Southsea - Oxford -
                    Birmingham
Southsea - Southampton - Frome - Bristol
Southsea - Southampton - Salisbury -
                    Bristol

Percentage of Scheduled Mileage
14.891%
Percentage of Revenue 13.981%

Greyhound Motor Services, Bristol

Greyhound was incorporated in February 1921 to take over the Coach business of Toogood & Bennett. A service was commenced between

Olympic Motor Services of 8 Kent Road, Southsea, operated twice daily to Bristol: one route via Salisbury and Frome, the other via Trowbridge and Bath. The company was purchased by Travellers Saloon Coaches, who had offices in Plymouth and Portsmouth, in 1932. They in turn sold out to Elliott Bros the following year. Olympic had owned two Gilfords with Weymann bodies, TP 9181/2. The former passed to Hants & Dorset and the latter to Western National when Elliott Bros was puirchased in 1935. (Senior Transport Archive)

Coach Stations

Above: *Up to 1939 the majority of the London services operated by the Pool continued on from Victoria Coach Station to terminate at the Terminal Coach Station, Clapham. This was used by Blue Belle Coaches whose services to the coast all departed at 9.45am: 15 minutes to go, according to the clock. The Red & White vehicle was due to leave at 10.05am. In 1937 Red & White purchased Blue Belle together with the coach station. (Keith Healey Collection)*

Below: *A typical prewar scene at Cheltenham, probably taken for the 2.00pm departure. The two Red & White Gloster coaches, No.* ***224*** *for Swansea and* ***227*** *for London have the revised livery for the coach fleet. (Keith Healey Collection)*

Bristol and London four years later on 10th February and it has been said this was the first express service to pick up and set down en route as well as at the termini. An extension of the service to Weston super Mare was introduced in 1929.

The Bristol Tramways and Carriage Co Ltd obtained financial control of Greyhound on 31st March 1928 but operated it as a separate company. Later in 1928 a Bristol - Torquay service was commenced with through bookings from London to the resort.

In January 1929 the Bristol - Weymouth service of Pioneer Motor Services (C F Russett) was acquired. Further expansion was made in 1930 with a joint service to Liverpool in conjunction with Merseyside Touring Company of that city. The last company to be taken over was in 1933 with the Bristol - London and Bristol - Torquay routes of Morning Star (E Jones). This brought about a pooling arrangement on the London routes with Elliott Bros of Bournemouth.

On 1st July 1934 Greyhound placed the following routes in the Pool. Although the two Liverpool services were shown in the original agreement they were later terminated at Bristol and Cheltenham northwards with the rest of the route being passed to Ribble Motor Services:

Paignton - Bristol - Gloucester - Birmingham
Paignton - Bristol - Shrewsbury - Liverpool
Ilfracombe - Bristol - Cheltenham - Liverpool
Bristol - Bath - Shaftesbury - Bournemouth
Bristol - Bath - Salisbury - Bournemouth
Bath - Bristol - Weston super Mare - Paignton
Bristol - Wells - Yeovil - Weymouth
Bristol - Evercreech - Wincanton - Weymouth

Percentage of Scheduled Mileage 10.695%
Percentage of Revenue 9.605%

Birmingham and Midland Motor Omnibus Co Ltd, known as Midland Red, Birmingham

Midland Red introduced its first express services southwestwards in 1921 with a 7½-hour journey, numbered 200, between Birmingham and Weston super Mare. By 1929 this timing had been reduced to 6 hours and renumbered X20. Other routes were also operated by that year to Bournemouth and Torquay, the latter interchanging at Bristol with Greyhound.

Apart from a financial interest in Black & White Motorways only one other purchase was made on a route to the South-West when, in 1933 and jointly with Greyhound, the Birmingham - Ilfracombe service of Brittons was acquired. The Traffic Commissioners refused to grant a new licence to the purchasers who had to be content that some competition had been removed from the route.

In July 1934 Midland Red placed the following routes into the Pool, the first two being feeders to connect with the other services:

Dudley - Worcester
Walsall - Birmingham
Birmingham - Oxford - Bournemouth
Birmingham - Weston super Mare
Birmingham - Bristol - Paignton

Percentage of Scheduled Mileage 9.777%
Percentage of Revenue 10.221%

United Counties Omnibus Co Ltd, Northampton

This Company was a latecomer to the negotiations; having purchased Allchin & Sons of Northampton in 1933, they were invited to join the discussions in January 1934.

The Allchin services to the southwest consisted of two routes: Northampton to Bournemouth via Oxford and Southampton with connections available to Portsmouth and Southsea, and Northampton to Torquay via Warwick and Bristol. There were other routes from Northampton to London, Hastings and Lowestoft but it was the network of feeder services to Northampton from Derby, Nottingham, Peterborough and Birmingham that were instrumental in enlarging the catchment area.

Prewar Scenes at Cheltenham

Above: Taken soon after the formation, this view shows the covered way and a fine selection of Pool and hired-in vehicles.

Below: A view taken in 1931 just after the coach station opened. Even in those days Black & White had to hire vehicles on busy days. In the foreground are two 2-ton Bristol 20-seaters, led by **HW 6031**. Alongside them is Bournemouth operator Shamrock & Rambler's **RU 8911**, a Daimler CF6 with Hall Lewis coachwork. (Both: Keith Healey Collection)

United Counties was also concentrating on the London route with the purchase of the Midland Motorways service from Northampton, which was co-ordinated with the ex-Allchin service.

In 1933 Eastern Counties had purchased Varsity Express and Varsity Coaches and under the territorial agreement transferred to United Counties in 1934 six vehicles and the Oxford - London service of Varsity Express.

When United Counties signed the agreement on joining the Pool a special clause was written in that no objection would be made by any of the Pool Members to the purchase by United Counties of the South Midland Motor Services route between Oxford and London.

In July 1934 the following services were placed in the Pool:

Northampton - Warwick - Torquay
Northampton - Bournemouth
Southampton - Southsea

Percentage of Scheduled Mileage 3.256%
Percentage of Revenue 3.409%

The Management Committee

How was the Pool to operate? The original scheduled mileage and receipts percentages have already been shown and certain routes were always operated by the same members.

Duplication was arranged by the staff of the Management Committee based at Cheltenham Coach Station, who had the full picture of bookings received. Member companies were approached for vehicle availability for the forthcoming summer season, then the non-member associated companies would be contacted, and finally certain independent companies. The cost of duplication was against the Pool and not to the member companies.

How were the routes to be licensed by the Traffic Commissioners? At the beginning of the Pool there was some confusion among the various Commissioners. The general principle was to licence each operator separately for each route operated. The North Western Chairman was not happy with this

arrangement and when six applications appeared before him for the Cardiff - Blackpool route he only granted the renewal of the Red & White licence, refusing the others. This reasoning was based on the fact that none of the operators would ever operate on the service so why grant a licence to them. In view of this no joint application was made for the London - Aberystwyth service licensed to Black & White. By 1936 the North Western Traffic Area was granting licences to all the Pool members but still a separate licence to each operator.

In October of that year a meeting was arranged between the Chairmen of various Traffic Areas and the Management Committee plus their Solicitors; after a great deal of discussion it was agreed that one licence for each route should be issued to Associated Motorways. The licence would name the constituent companies operating jointly that were trading under that name. Although in the 1950s and 60s this arrangement was challenged by new Chairmen of the various Traffic Areas it was never changed until the formation of National Travel in 1974.

Prior to the commencement of the Second World War in 1939 Road Service Licences were issued and renewable each year. All the Pool services were subject to scrutiny by the main line railways and meetings had to be arranged each year when discussions would take place between the Pool and the railways. From the beginning the railways had given the scheme their "negative approval", a phrase used at the first Traffic Court hearing. It is recorded that they used to start discussions by declaration of "non-approval" to the services as a whole. The yearly negotiations though at times hard were always conducted in a friendly and helpful spirit as the railways came to see the economy of the scheme. It will be seen later how the introduction of various services or timings were blocked by the railways which meant the Pool having to wait for a few years until the time was more opportune. However, in the 1960s the railways seemed to make a comeback and persuaded Traffic Commissioners, especially in Yorkshire, that duplication restrictions were needed on new services to protect the rail system.

Midland Red and Great Western

Above: *Midland Red* **HA 4999** *was a 1930 SOS RR-type chassis with Brush/Carlyle 29-seat coachwork. The body and registration number had come from an earlier SOS XL type. It is seen arriving at Cheltenham from Birmingham in August 1934. The vehicle was withdrawn in 1943. (Keith Healey Collection)*

Below: MY 2049 was a Leyland Tiger, bodied by Dodson, in the Great Western Express fleet. Great Western was the leading operator on the London to South Wales services, having started with a day service to Cardiff in October 1928, adding a night run from March 1929. The owner, Gerry Nowell, had a flair for publicity and launched the new night service by having the Houston Sisters, of vaudeville fame, baptise the coach with a bottle of champagne. Named "The Welsh Midnight", the vehicles on this service were equipped with "underfloor heating" and the seats had lace headrests. In June 1929 more than 3,500 passengers were carried of whom 800 used the night service. (Keith Healey Collection)

Tourist of Southampton

Tourist Motor Coaches, of Southampton, could trace its origins back to 1919 when B H Ransom established a coach business in the city. A limited company was formed in 1927 and a daily express service between Southampton and London commenced, with certain journeys extended to and from Bournemouth. In 1930 Tourist started a Southampton to Liverpool service; although they applied under the new regulations to extend the service to Bournemouth, they were unsuccessful and passengers to and from that resort had to change at Southampton. In 1935 Tourist sold out to Thomas Tilling. Shown are No. **25 (TR 6355)**, a 1929 Albion PKB26 with 26-seat coach body, and 1931 20-seat Leyland Cub No. **39 (TR 9920)**, a very early (chassis number 16) KP1 model. After the sale of Tourist, 36 vehicles were divided among Western National, Southern National and Hants & Dorset and these two became Southern National 3532/8. (Both: Keith Healey Collection)

Bonneted Luxury

Above: In late 1928, Mr N D Reyne, of Austral Garage, Stroud, was operating a daily service to Gloucester as well as twice daily to London. At the same time, E Grey & Sons were operating under the fleetname "Red & Black" between London and Oxford, later extended to Gloucester. Mr Reyne, an Australian, had served in the Royal Flying Corps during the war. In 1932 he formed Red Bus Services and it is believed that by that time he had purchased the Red & Black route. His trade mark was a kangaroo on the sides of his vehicles. Reyne became a director of Red & White when his business was purchased by the latter in 1933. (Keith Healey Collection)

Below: Links Safety Coaches, of Bournemouth, operated a daily service from that resort to Birmingham via a similar route to that used by Midland Red. The service was purchased by Black & White in 1933, giving the latter a new picking-up point in Reading, a town not previously served by them and which was quickly brought into the Cheltenham connecting facility. Three Studebaker Highway coaches were taken over, one of which is shown here. (Keith Healey Collection)

Finally, there was the brand image to sell the services. None of the original Management Committee could remember who suggested "Associated", they all agreed it should be something "Motorways" because of the Black & White involvement. Various names were suggested: "Associated" had a nice ring about it, and thus was born Associated Motorways.

For publicity purposes a colour scheme of orange, green and black was used in cutouts and posters; vehicles were always shown in these colours. All Traffic and Agent's bulletins were printed in green ink while the letterhead for correspondence was printed in green on a yellow paper. A coach was used for the symbol: originally a front view based on an ex-South Wales Express AEC. After the war an offside view of a Willowbrook-bodied Black & White was used, and finally a Bristol/ECW coach.

The Years 1935 - 1942

In 1935 the first change to the structure of the Pool was made with the purchase by Thomas Tilling of the Elliott Bros company. The express licences were transferred to either Western or Southern National, while the excursion licences in Bournemouth passed to Hants & Dorset Motor Services, another Tilling Associated Company. At the same time, Tourist Motor Coaches of Southampton was also purchased with the services being distributed on the same lines as those of Elliott Bros.

These purchases brought the Members of the Pool up to seven with Elliott Bros being replaced by Western and Southern National; for mileage and receipts purposes the latter were treated as one company, taking over the ex-Elliott entitlement, shown as Royal Blue, which the National companies had decided to retain as a brand name. It is rather surprising that the opportunity was not taken to combine all the Royal Blue services with the Pool routes, as originally Western National had taken part in talks on the co-ordination scheme. There must have been advantages in elimination of certain dead mileage where common destinations were served; at times, too, a clash of interests between Royal Blue and the Pool was inevitable.

*Black & White **DF 7555**, a 1929 Leyland Tiger TS2, with Leyland 26-seat coachwork, is seen in pre-Pool days heading for Birmingham. The vehicle behind was **DG 767**, a London Lorries-bodied machine dating from 1930. It also had 26 seats and both vehicles were to dual-doorway specification, a safety requirement of local licensing authorities. (Keith Healey Collection)*

New Bristols and Rebodied AECs

Above: An official view, taken when the vehicle was brand new, is believed to be of a Bristol B-type - one of the last examples, sporting the modernised radiator that subsequently appeared on the J-type chassis from Bristol. This 30-seater was delivered to Greyhound in 1931. Towns served by the company were signwritten (or perhaps transfers were used) onto the louvres above the vehicle's side windows. (Keith Healey Collection)

Below: In 1934 the Eastern Counties Omnibus Co transferred to United Counties the Oxford - London service of Varsity Express, together with six vehicles, which they had purchased the year before. **VE 3031**, an AEC Regal, was rebodied by Burlingham in 1939. (Keith Healey Collection)

Prewar Cubs and Tigers

Above: *In 1933 Black & White purchased four Leyland Cubs with 20-seat Duple coachwork, of which **DG 6559** is shown. The Cubs were used mainly on day excursions and private hire but at times of need appeared on Pool workings. (Keith Healey Collection)*

Below: *A publicity postcard of a new Leyland Tiger TS7 with Burlingham 32-seat rear-entrance coachwork. This vehicle - of which the correct registration was **DK 9879** and not that shown - was the first diesel-engined coach for Yelloway Motor Services. The "via" indicator was to be amended to read Cheltenham instead of Gloucester although Bristol was retained. (D Haddock Collection)*

Leyland Tigers

*Above: A further view of **TF 9100**, the Leyland Motors Lion LT5 demonstrator superbly finished in Black & White livery. (Senior Transport Archive/BCVM)*

Below: One of the 1929 Leyland TS2 Tigers, regrettably unidentifiable, seen in as-built condition with body by London Lorries Ltd with roof rack and - at that date - Black & White's pre-Pool livery. (Keith Healey Collection)

City of Oxford

Taken at Nottingham in 1949, these photographs show two 1939 City of Oxford AEC Regals,
HFC 410/2, *fitted with Weymann's dual-purpose bodywork. The vehicles were clearly on hire to help
out on Pool services, although no other record can be found of this hiring; it must have been of some
duration to justify the unique large printed "On Hire to BLACK & WHITE Motorways Ltd" labels.*
(Both: G H F Atkins)

Second-hand Coaches

Above: EFC 297, one of the 1936 City of Oxford Weymann-bodied dual-purpose AEC Regals, is seen at Nottingham in Black & White livery in 1950. (Keith Healey Collection)

*Below: Lined up at Cheltenham are the six 1936 AEC Regals - **EFC 294-9** - purchased from City of Oxford in 1950 to augment the fleet once new Bristol chassis were unavailable to Black & White following Bristol's move into state ownership. The AECs ran only two seasons and all six were sold at the end of the 1951 summer season. Ten second-hand Dennis Lancet 2s were also purchased - from South Wales Transport - by Black & White at the same time; they were also sold in 1951. (S N J White)*

In 1936 the Pool proposed two new routes: Cheltenham via Oxford, St Albans and Enfield to London; and Birmingham via Hereford and Carmarthen to Tenby. Objections by other operators prevented both. The same year saw the end of the direct London to Aberystwyth service, passengers now having to change at Cheltenham. The winding up of Greyhound Motor Services by its parent company meant all licences were now granted under the name of Bristol Tramways & Carriage Co Ltd, but "Greyhound" was retained as a brand name for Bristol's express services. Prior to the Pool Black & White had proposed a Cheltenham - Bedford route, because of objections the idea was dropped but arrangements were made for through bookings via Oxford to Buckingham and Bedford on the service operated by G O Gammond of Bedford. This arrangement continued until the operator was purchased by City of Oxford Motor Services in January 1942.

The type of operation not anticipated by the Road Traffic Act was the introduction of seven- and eight-day centre holidays where the hotel and excursions at the resort were included in the price and the coach stayed with the party all the time. It was generally considered that the extended tours should be of the progressive type using several hotels and resorts during the week. The express service operators objected to the centre holidays on the grounds that passengers should travel on their services. This, of course, affected the Pool but licences were generally granted as many operators had run tours prior to 1930. The Traffic Commissioners did make one condition on granting licences and this related to the number of excursions to be operated from the resort. These licences became known as "fantails" with the "feathers" being the excursions. Only one excursion, or feather, was granted on which the operator could use his own coach, all the other excursions had to be "on hire" to a local operator. In the sixties tour operators were purchasing their own hotels and successfully appealed for a further feather on the grounds that they were now ratepayers and had an interest in bringing business to the resort.

In 1937 the Pool, in conjunction with Ribble, Yelloway and North Western, introduced a series of inclusive holidays at nine resorts with passengers travelling by its services; the price included hotel and excursions - if you can't beat them, join them! Booking Agents were controlled by the member company in whose area they were situated. All South Wales Agents came under Red & White who also at that time undertook the booking control of the Pool services in the London area, as London Coastal was unable to cope with it at that time. Most London services terminated at Clapham Coach Station where connecting services were offered by Blue Belle Coaches to the South East Coast. In 1937 Red & White purchased the Company as well as the property so it was usual for Red & White Agents to book connections via Clapham rather than Victoria.

The ex-Tourist Southampton - Liverpool service was placed in the Pool from 1st January 1938 by Southern National. However, because of pending licensing applications the licence was not transferred to the Pool until the following year. 1938 saw the purchase by Midland Red of two Companies, G H Burnham and P Owen & Sons, both of whom operated in the Bromsgrove and Stourport areas with services to Blackpool and Aberystwyth. Burnham also operated to Weston super Mare. Under the signed agreement these routes were offered to the Pool by Midland Red but because the licences were restricted and difficulty in obtaining certified figures of operation the offer was declined.

Prior to 1932 the Great Western Railway operated a coach service between Cheltenham and Oxford to connect with the London trains. In that year the service was transferred to Black & White who immediately passed it to Bristol Tramways for operation. By 1938 Bristol wished to extend the service in Oxford to terminate at Gloucester Green bus station and an arrangement was reached with the Pool whereby Bristol would pay the Pool 25% of the fares of passengers travelling to or from Burford, Northleach and Cheltenham to the new terminus.

Although night services had always been operated on the South Wales routes it was not until 1938 that special night services for the August Bank Holiday period were operated

War and its Aftermath

*Above: In 1941 eight coaches were hired by the Pool from the East Kent Road Car Co. Park Royal-bodied 32-seat Leyland Tiger TS8 **JG 9940**, dating from 1938, was one of them; it is seen at Victoria Coach Station operating a relief journey to Cheltenham with a Black & White Bristol behind. The vehicles were returned to East Kent in 1942. (Bus & Coach)*

*Below: When the express services restarted in 1946 anything that could run, ran. This 1949 picture shows the 18-year-old Leyland TS1 **TR 9922** that had begun life with Tourist Coaches, Southampton, and passed to Elliott Bros in 1933; moving on to Southern National in 1935, the vehicle was rebodied in 1939. It is seen during a tea-break stop while operating as a relief car on the 2.00pm departure from Cheltenham to Bournemouth. (Keith Healey)*

from Derby, Birmingham and Nottingham to Bournemouth, Southsea and Paignton. The following year saw a strike by Royal Blue road staff between 1st and 14th May and it was recorded that the mileage obligations of Royal Blue were covered as best as possible.

The outbreak of the Second World War on 3rd September 1939 brought about the suspension of all night services from 7th September. By the 10th a total of 39 scheduled services had been withdrawn, as had the Birmingham - Weston super Mare and Cardiff - Blackpool services; all journeys which were of a purely holiday character and the inclusive holiday-centre arrangements were also suspended. Fuel rationing was introduced on 23rd September and for the winter service commencing 1st October the scheduled mileage was reduced by 26%. Again, in 1940 the mileage was further reduced and the original proposal to the recently renamed Regional Transport Commissioners (the former Chairmen of Traffic Commissioners) was to operate 75% of the normal schedule. However, the RTC wanted a further reduction and suggested no more than 50% of the 1939 scheduled mileage. In the end 44% of the scheduled and duplicate mileage was authorised.

For the 1940 summer service fuel was allocated on the basis of estimates and claims to cover 1,251,242 miles were made, in fact 1,255,672 miles were operated. At the same time Black & White took over all Midland Red service and duplicate mileage as well as their own, this lasting until the withdrawal of all the routes in 1942.

It was agreed that fuel coupons for stage and express services should be allocated to the licence-holder and this meant that the Pool was responsible for the operating of the services within the fuel restrictions given to them, not the member companies. This enabled them in 1941 to hire from East Kent Road Car Company eight vehicles to assist in the operations.

However, the Regional Transport Commissioners were placing various restrictions and asking express operators to withdraw routes. Principally, the Pool was concerned with cross-country routes where there were no rail or local services. The need

for the services was shown by the traffic carried in 1941, the last full year of operations: although heavily restricted, the revenue received was the highest since the commencement of the Pool. The fares were the same in 1941 as they had been in 1934.

In the end all express services still running were suspended on Government orders from 1st October 1942, but November saw the commencement of a Western National service between Bournemouth and Trowbridge numbered 405, which replaced a Pool service between the two towns and was operated by the Royal Blue coach fleet.

Ribble and Yelloway 1929 - 1939

The story of Associated Motorways is not complete without reference to the two companies in the northwest, Ribble Motor Services of Preston and Yelloway Motor Services of Rochdale, which over the years booked thousands of passengers on the Pool services.

The services to the southwest from Liverpool commenced in the late 1920s when various small coach companies operated to Torquay and Bournemouth. The main operator was the Merseyside Touring Company who had come to an agreement with Greyhound Motor Services of Bristol in 1930 to operate a joint service to Paignton as well as Weston super Mare. The latter route was revised and extended to Ilfracombe in the following year.

The services from Manchester followed the same pattern with the principal operator being the reformed Holt Bros of Rochdale, which became Yelloway in 1932. Both Yelloway and Merseyside provided connections at Bristol, interchanging passengers with other Greyhound routes. Yelloway also connected at Gloucester with Red & White and at Taunton with Lavender Blue.

When discussions took place in 1932 on the co-ordination of routes, Ribble was invited to participate as Merseyside had now been fully merged with Ribble. There was one slight problem as far as Liverpool was concerned and this was the Red & White activity in the area. The Company had come to a working agreement with MacShanes Motor Services

Rare Sightings

*Above: A 1949 view at Bournemouth illustrates one of the four AEC Q types from the Elliott Bros fleet that had passed to Hants & Dorset in 1935. **LJ 8600** retained the Royal Blue livery and fleetname until 1937 but was by 1949 in a green and cream colour scheme. (Keith Healey)*

*Below: Before 1956, when the direct Cheltenham to Eastbourne service commenced, connecting facilities were available at Hilsea between the Pool and the South Coast Express, which was jointly operated by Royal Blue, Southdown and East Kent. Seen in this 1950 view at Eastbourne is Southdown **UF 9779**, a 1933 Leyland Tiger TS4 with Harrington 32-seat coachwork, operating a relief journey from Portsmouth. (Keith Healey)*

who operated amongst other routes a service to Torquay. MacShane, to put it mildly, was a wily old bird, as the author knows from dealings with him during the 1960s.

In the end Red & White had to purchase a controlling interest in the company from December 1932. The year before they had also obtained a controlling interest in Samuelsons Saloon Coaches, operating between Liverpool and London. This route connected at Birmingham with the Red & White service to Gloucester and South Wales and also at Oxford with South Midland to Portsmouth. 1933 saw the transfer of the Nell Gwynne Cardiff - Liverpool and Blackpool licences to Red & White. Negotiations were taking place to purchase the Liverpool - Newcastle on Tyne service of Tyne Mersey Services and application was made for a Liverpool - Manchester service via the newly opened East Lancashire Road. Finally they purchased an interest in the All British Line, which also operated between Liverpool and London with a connecting service from Chester to North Wales. So here was a company that, with slight alteration to its licences, could control the Liverpool area for services to the southwest and South Wales. In fact Red & White was finding it difficult to operate this group of services and, in early 1934, came to an agreement with Ribble and Crosville to surrender all its licences in Liverpool with the exception of the ex-Nell Gwynne route, in return receiving £5,000 for the goodwill of the routes. This made it easier for them to become part of the proposed Pool.

Back in 1932 Ribble had indicated that they did not want to continue their joint services to Torquay and Ilfracombe if the proposal for a Cheltenham interchange took place and would terminate their services at Cheltenham and Bristol respectively. The first move was to change the lunch and tea halts from Tewkesbury to Cheltenham on the Ilfracombe service for the 1933 season. Application was then made to terminate the service at Cheltenham for the 1934 season and also to operate the service throughout the year. At the same time the Paignton service would be retimed to depart Liverpool at midday and would terminate at Bristol. The other operators were not happy with the Bristol terminus and

considered that it should operate as far as Cheltenham. Red & White also objected, as the timings would clash with the ex-Nell Gwynne service between Liverpool and Hereford, which was common ground. Ribble amended the application so that after leaving Chester it joined the Cheltenham route at Wellington (Salop). The Traffic Commissioners granted the Ilfracombe variation to terminate at Cheltenham but refused throughout-the-year operation. They also refused the revised timetable on the Paignton service so Ribble continued to operate to Paignton in 1934, but not jointly with Greyhound as in 1933, while they awaited the result of their appeals against the Traffic Commissioners' decisions. This came in time for the 1935 season with the Minister granting the revised timetable and route to Bristol but upholding the original decision that the Cheltenham service should operate in the summer season only.

The Yelloway service continued its original route offering connections at Gloucester and Bristol, this time with the Pool as the connecting Company. In March 1936 discussions took place with the Pool for the service to be rerouted into Cheltenham and from 22nd August 1936 Yelloway vehicles appeared in Cheltenham. The Pool produced a special connecting leaflet for the Company and showed the link on its route map. On the outbreak of the Second World War Ribble and Yelloway withdrew their services for the duration.

Restarting and Route Expansion 1946 - 1964

With the invasion of Europe in 1944 by the Allies, Management Committee thoughts were turning to the resumption of services. Their main concern was that there could be changes in licensing procedures and express services might not receive the same consideration as before the war. On 1st November of that year application was made to the Regional Transport Commissioners to resume all services. The RTC stated that the time was not yet ripe and the applications were held in abeyance.

In 1945 Red & White United Transport, the Holding Company, purchased South Midland

Regals and Tigers

Above: Southern National/Royal Blue AEC Regal No. **1063** (**ETA 997**) *and two others are seen leaving Digbeth coach station. The vehicles are empty and the clock suggests that they had just finished duplicating the 9.30am from Bournemouth on a summer Saturday. Royal Blue had operated that service since 1929, purchasing the following year the Pathfinder service operating between Plymouth and Birmingham. (Keith Healey Collection)*

Below: The parking area behind Bournemouth bus station in 1949 found Southern National/Royal Blue ex-Devon General **DV 5480** having just completed a duplicate run on the 2.00pm service from Cheltenham. The 1930 vehicle had been purchased from Devon General by Southern National in 1935 with a service-bus body; it was rebodied as a coach in 1936, entering the Royal Blue fleet in that year. (Keith Healey)*

*<< **Opposite page:** BAD 637* with Burlingham 30-seat coachwork was one of a batch of eight delivered in 1936 as the first Bristol LO6Gs in the Black & White fleet. It is seen outside Marshall's booking office in Huntingdon Street, Nottingham, in April 1936 in the course of a publicity tour before going into service. The deep seats and side curtains call out for passengers to travel by coach; the roof rack blends in with the flow of the coachwork: coaching at its best. (G H F Atkins)

Above: Greyhound **FHT 781** with Duple 32-seat body was of a type often seen on Pool services, mainly from Bristol, over the years. (R N Hannay)

Below: Red & White was famous for its Duple-bodied Albion coaches. **CWO 413** is seen approaching London with a full load in the postwar period; all the Pool services now terminated at Victoria instead of at Clapham. (R Marshall Collection)

Motor Services, which continued to be operated under its own name. This made it difficult for the two services operated, Worcester - Oxford - London and Oxford - Southsea to be transferred to the Pool, as they were the core of South Midland's operation.

Before any services could be commenced there was the question of fares to be charged as the present fare scale did not account for the increase that had been made in other sectors of the industry. After long discussions between operators and the Commissioners an overall increase of 16.66% was agreed. This enabled the Pool to recommence operation on 3rd June 1946 on 14 routes with one journey per day in each direction. In the same year an application was lodged for a Cheltenham - Tenby service. The RTC insisted on a maximum speed of 15mph in urban areas and 20mph in rural areas; the Pool felt that such restrictions would prejudice the selling of the service and withdrew the application.

The demand for coach travel in 1947 exceeded the supply of vehicles but it did see the introduction of non-stop through coaches from Birmingham and Coventry to various southwest coastal resorts.

There were also changes in the financial structure of companies, with Thomas Tilling in 1947 selling all their interests in bus companies to the newly formed British Transport Commission. This included Pool members Western National, Southern National, Bristol Tramways and United Counties. Three years later Red & White United Transport also sold out to the BTC. During the winter of 1947/8 Black & White took over the scheduled mileage in the Pool of both Midland Red and Greyhound.

Early in 1948 applications were being made mainly by independent operators for licences to carry military personnel from camps to distant terminals. The Pool was concerned with applications from the Salisbury area to many destinations served by them. After various court hearings the Traffic Commissioners ruled that licences would be granted to convey personnel to the nearest railheads, which were clearly defined, Bristol being the nearest rail head for Wiltshire Camps. Fuel was still rationed and vehicles had to be hired to cover the services that could be operated. In 1948 members operated five million miles with another million being run by hired vehicles. As well as the military camp services independent coach operators were applying for services to the coast, especially from the Midlands during the peak summer season. Although the Pool, with other associated companies, always objected, many licences were granted because of the inability of the established operators to carry any additional traffic at certain times. The Pool always put forward the argument that passengers could travel on Friday or Sunday if there was no room on Saturdays; the Traffic Commissioners responded that as hotel bookings were from Saturday to Saturday people had no choice and generally speaking the public must come first. The Pool reintroduced centre holidays based on their services to coastal resorts. Ribble had offered holidays northwards before the war and now extended the scope of destinations to include not only Blackpool but also the Lake District and the Isle of Man marketed under the name of "Easyway" holidays. This two-way traffic helped to boost the Pool revenue.

Over the next few years new services were added. 1952 saw the commencement of a Cambridge - Cheltenham via Bedford route. Objection to the service had been made by Premier Travel on the grounds that the joint service with Percivals between Cambridge and Oxford offered adequate connections at Oxford to Cheltenham. They even appealed against the Traffic Commissioners decision but were unsuccessful and also lost their appeal against the decision not to grant them a service between Cambridge and Torquay.

A new service between Cheltenham and Bridport later extended to Exmouth was commenced. This had its origins in a joint Greyhound, Royal Blue service between Bristol and Bridport, which had been transferred to the Pool. This service had commenced in July 1938 and operated mainly through the Pool area. The Cheltenham - Cardiff service was extended to Barry on one timing in conjunction with Western Welsh. Local operators had also opposed the new Cheltenham - Tenby service, which commenced in 1952 after a Traffic Court hearing.

Hand-Painted Messages

The South Wales services from Cheltenham served so many destinations that each Red & White vehicle entering the coach station on a busy day had, usually on the window of the sliding door, whitewash-painted lists of the towns it was serving. In the upper picture **HWO 359**, a 33-seater, is going to "Lydney, Chepstow, Newport, Cardiff only" whilst 31-seat **GWO 874** (below) is bound for "All stops to Chepstow and past Neath". These Albion CX39 coaches were new in May 1950 and February 1949 and were withdrawn in 1964/59. (Both: R Marshall Collection)

The application to operate the Southampton - Liverpool service in the winter was not successful and was withdrawn after objections were made by Ribble and the railways. Another application not granted was for a Stevenage - Cheltenham service in which the railways, as the principal objector, argued that the application was too ambitious; although the decision was taken to Appeal, the Minister agreed with the Traffic Commissioners. Later, United Counties attempted to obtain a Stevenage - Oxford service but again without success. Perhaps the Commissioners saw through the scheme of linking at Oxford, as it had been the intention, if granted, to place the service in the Pool.

Night services were introduced from the Midlands over three different routes to connect at 2.30am on Saturday and Sunday mornings with services to Bournemouth, Ilfracombe, Paignton and Exeter for Cornwall, returning from the resorts on Friday and Saturday evenings. Through-running in conjunction with Southdown Motor Services between Bristol, Brighton and Eastbourne was also commenced.

In 1954 the 4.30pm Cheltenham - Weston super Mare journey was extended to Torquay. The railways had opposed this for many years, however despite their objections the service was granted by the Traffic Commissioners. This brought for the first time Torquay and Paignton into the range of services available from Yorkshire via Birmingham with through vehicles being operated at weekends. In many cases the Pool was the only operator on certain sections of a route and it was agreed by the Western, East Midland and South Wales Commissioners that subject to local conditions passengers could be picked up and set down anywhere on the authorised route.

Nineteen-fifty-four was a year that will be remembered by all the Pool booking agents for the introduction of the "Universal" type ticket and doing away with the ruling of one ticket per passenger. Now up to four passengers could be booked on the same ticket. The Liverpool - Southampton route was at last licensed to operate through to Bournemouth although objections were made by centre tour operators in the North-West. Proof was given of the number of passengers who already

changed at Southampton for Bournemouth but the Traffic Commissioners imposed a duplication restriction on the licence, which did not help very much.

Two new services were opened in 1955 with the commencement by Lincolnshire Road Car of a journey from Scunthorpe to Cheltenham via Lincoln and Grantham and by Eastern Counties between Great Yarmouth and Cheltenham via Norwich and Cambridge. After a year's operation the two licences were transferred to the Pool with Lincolnshire and Eastern Counties surrendering their licences and becoming full members of the Pool thus bringing its membership up to nine. Crosville also made application for a Bangor - Cheltenham service via Caernarfon and Welshpool but so strong was the railway opposition that it was withdrawn.

A rail strike from 28th May to 14th June involved an extra 220 vehicles being operated during the strike as against the same period in 1954. The number of passengers carried during 1955 passed the two million mark, which was appropriate for its 21st year of operations, but it was another seven years before that total was again achieved.

The Midland General Omnibus Company was considering applying for licences to operate through services from Mansfield to Torquay and Bournemouth. After a meeting, also attended by the Trent Motor Traction Company, the Pool suggested the Cheltenham - Nottingham service be extended to Mansfield and Midland General, together with Trent, could provide vehicles on hire to the Pool for the weekend through service. Another suggestion was for the companies to jointly apply for a service to Cheltenham, the route to be discussed, and if the application were successful it would be taken into the Pool. In the end neither Trent nor Midland General applied for any services and the Pool was granted the extension to Mansfield.

The Pool also applied for a service between Felixstowe and Cheltenham via Ipswich, Colchester and Hertford. Although a licence was granted in full by the Western Traffic Commissioners, the other Areas imposed so many restrictions that it was impracticable to take the grant up. There was no such problem for the joint Pool and Southdown service

Midland Red

Above: Black & White, as well as being the principal partner in the Pool, also operated day and extended tours, and private hire, from Cheltenham. Each summer, to cover these commitments, vehicles were hired from associated companies to operate on pool services, thus releasing Black & White's best vehicles for tour and private work. Midland Red **FHA 412**, an SOS ONC with Duple body, by then 20 years old, was one of ten hired in 1959. It is seen leaving Cheltenham coach station. *(Keith Healey Collection)*

Below: Originally intended for extended tour work, for which it had a 26-seat Duple body, Midland Red **KHA 355**, a C2 type, had its seating increased to 30 in 1954. In this view it was showing Paignton as its destination. *(John Fozard Collection)*

between Cheltenham and Eastbourne/ Brighton, which commenced in 1956.

The Suez Crisis, which had started just before Christmas 1956, began to take effect and from 1st January 1957 only 60% of the normal winter timetable could be operated. The Government also imposed an additional tax on fuel, but licensed operators were allowed a blanket surcharge on their fares of 1/12th to be removed when the crisis ended. The fuel rationing scheme ended in April and restrictions on bookings for the summer season at 70% of normal capacity was lifted. Unfortunately the Government did not remove all the additional tax on fuel as promised and it was necessary to bring in a fare increase from April 24th, the day after the 1/12th surcharge finished. This brought about a four-tier fare table: Winter, Monday-Friday Summer, Friday nights and Saturdays Summer, Sundays and Bank Holidays Summer - an Agent's nightmare. Certain services were withdrawn including the night services from the south-west coast on Fridays to Cheltenham and the corresponding services southwards on Sunday mornings at 2.30pm, as well as their connecting services from the Midlands to Cheltenham. Alterations were made to other services with the Shrewsbury service being extended to Llandudno at weekends thus avoiding the change at Birmingham. The Corby service was also extended to Peterborough.

An exchange of routes took place between the Pool and Greyhound, Royal Blue. The 7.00am Cheltenham - London via Stroud, returning at 5.15pm, had received only poor support and the route was transferred to the Bristol - London Pool and commenced from Stroud instead of Cheltenham. In return the Pool received the Greyhound service between Stroud and Minehead, which had been originally offered to the Pool in 1934 and refused. This service was retimed to commence from Cheltenham.

As if the Suez Crisis was not enough there was a general nationwide strike of company bus crews during the month of July from the 20th to the 28th, but the final blow came in September with an outbreak of Asian flu, although this did not affect the Pool as much as it did the stage carriage operators. All these factors produced a drop of over half a million passenger journeys compared to 1956.

In an effort to attract additional traffic, special leaflets were produced for the first time showing in detail the connecting facilities available at London Victoria Coach Station to destinations served by East Kent, Eastern National and Maidstone & District. In the same vein, through bookings were available via Cambridge on a range of destinations on routes operated by Eastern Counties and again fully detailed leaflets were issued. Coach/air services to the Channel Islands were also introduced in conjunction with Jersey Airlines from Hurn and Exeter Airports. The proposed extension in South Wales to Milford Haven produced railway objections and was not proceeded with but the Tenby service was successfully extended to Pembroke and Pembroke Dock. South Wales Transport had purchased the extended tour business of Wye Valley Motors of Hereford and the Pool introduced on behalf of South Wales additional journeys from Hereford to Blackpool serving Harlands Hotel on Queens Promenade, the journeys to be operated as and when required.

It had always been Pool policy to accept bookings up to the departure of the coach except on certain peak weekends when stop notices were issued, this being mainly due to duplication restrictions. In some circumstances it did mean having to find an extra vehicle at short notice. However, the Pool was quite happy with the arrangements. In 1959 they made checks on how many passengers made late bookings and discovered over one hundred thousand passengers had booked under these conditions, showing that the trend in late bookings had increased. These would have been lost if the 24-hour rule, which existed with other companies, had been enforced.

The first 36ft-long coach to depart from London Victoria Coach Station had to be a Pool vehicle: a Black & White Leyland Leopard with a Plaxton body left Victoria for South Wales on 30th March 1962. The M5 and M50 (Ross Spur) were the first of the new motorways to involve Pool services, resulting in a direct service between Birmingham and Cardiff on 21st July 1962; although the mileage was only seven miles different from

Black & White Prewar Bristols

*Seen in London in the 1950s, shortly before their withdrawal, are Black & White **BAD 635** (above), one of the first Bristol JO6Gs (with Burlingham 30-seat coachwork), delivered to the company in 1936; and (below) one of the 1940 Duple-bodied L6G 31-seaters. These vehicles were withdrawn respectively in 1954 and 1959. The Company had a high regard for the Bristol chassis and reordered them after the war, only to be quickly denied that opportunity following the restriction placed on Bristol by which it could supply only state-owned companies. (S N J White; Keith Healey Collection)*

the route via Cheltenham, 98 minutes were knocked off the running time, and waiting time at Cheltenham while changing vehicles was also eliminated.

Many of the passengers carried by the Pool made their journeys in the summer but with services operating daily throughout the year winter travel can become a problem and the Winter of 1962/3 was no exception. The South-West was hit by a blizzard on 29th December, which in four hours produced 15-20ft snow drifts in exposed places. Two Pool vehicles were involved among many others. A Black & White travelling to Weymouth became stuck in snow drifts on Wardon Hill at an altitude of 780ft. Its occupants, and those from a Royal Blue vehicle operating Exeter - Bournemouth, sought safety in a café. Two days later such was the condition of some passengers that three Navy helicopters were used to ferry nineteen people to hospital; the remaining passengers were taken by Army half-track vehicles across country to safety.

The second incident involved a Royal Blue coach operating from Cheltenham to Bournemouth, which was brought to a halt near East Knoyle in Wiltshire. The passengers were conveyed by four-wheel drive vehicles to a public house where they stayed for two days before being rescued. Blizzards and then icy roads continued throughout January into early February, after which conditions improved.

The 1963 summer season saw not only a direct service between Birmingham and Minehead but at last the commencement jointly with Crosville Motor Services of the Cheltenham - Bangor route. A new service between Cheltenham and Swanage via Swindon and Corfe Castle, together with a night connection from Norwich to Cheltenham for the 2.30am Saturday departures, completed the year.

Ribble and Yelloway 1946 - 1964

Yelloway recommenced operations in 1946 after the war had ended but still on their prewar timings. By 1949 they had successfully applied for a daily service though still restricted to summer-only operation.

Ribble recommenced the following year on May 11th but in time for the 1948 season had added a Friday night service to Cheltenham. Meanwhile the Pool had applied for a 2.30am departure on summer Saturdays to Bournemouth and Ilfracombe. These timings were not shown in the Pool timetable and were exclusively for traffic brought into Cheltenham by the Ribble and Yelloway Friday night services. Through vehicles were operated by Yelloway with the vehicles returning on Saturday mornings. Crews were generally changed over at Bristol or in the case of hired vehicles a second driver travelled down on the Friday day service to take over on the Saturday. There seems to be a doubt as to whether Ribble operated across Cheltenham at that time, all passengers having to change there.

Both Ribble and Yelloway were having to refuse passengers on certain weekends because of shortage of vehicles as well as fuel rationing. In May 1947 Yelloway had placed an advert in newspapers to the effect that they were unable to book any more passengers to or from Torquay, Bournemouth and Ilfracombe on Saturday or Sunday for the rest of the summer season.

By 1951 the position had eased but Yelloway still had to restrict its operation to a maximum of 18 vehicles south on a Friday night and 17 on Saturday mornings. Of that number three vehicles on Friday evening and eight on Saturday mornings were allocated for Pool connections. Both companies applied to increase the timings by operating a summer Saturday night service southwards with an additional night service northwards on Friday and Saturdays, Ribble as far as Cheltenham and Yelloway to Torquay.

At the same time the Pool extended its night services for the 1952 season to connect with these services. They also introduced an additional service to Torquay, which connected at Exeter with the revised Royal Blue timings to Cornwall departing at 8.00am. This brought about new destinations that could not hitherto be reached by passengers from the North-West without an overnight stop en route. North of Liverpool Ribble, in conjunction with Western SMT and Scottish Omnibuses, had revised their services to Scotland enabling through bookings to be made via Liverpool to all points on the Pool

Postwar Bristols

Above: In 1948 Royal Blue received the first delivery of new postwar vehicles, of which Brisol L **JUO 932** was one. The front-entrance Duple body, complete with roof rack, had 31 seats. Clem Preece ("Mr Royal Blue") was so keen to see the new vehicles that he walked five miles out of Exeter to meet them on delivery. (S N J White)

Below: In 1949 Black & White were receiving their last Bristol chassis, as the manufacturer was henceforth unable to supply to non-state-owned companies. Although based on the normal L6G chassis, they were fitted with fully fronted Duple coachwork with 30 seats, as demonstrated by **JDD 495**. The following year saw the company forced to purchase second-hand vehicles while it looked for an alternative chassis supplier. (G H F Atkins)

network. A special booklet was issued under the promotional name of "Westlinks".

By 1953 Ribble had applied to operate throughout the year this time being successful. Yelloway also made a similar application to operate a winter service originally to Bristol later revised to Cheltenham and this commenced operation in time for Easter 1954.

Ribble had always carried heavy traffic from Bristol northwards on its 8.45am departure with through vehicles to Blackpool and connections onwards to the Lake District. In 1954 Ribble introduced a further service this time originating in Bristol leaving at 11.30pm on Friday evenings and terminating at Liverpool (Pier Head), returning from that point at 12.50pm on Saturdays, operating during the summer season. The route had a separate licence from that of the Liverpool - Bristol service with its own vehicle allowance and extra timings were provided for the Bristol Co-op Society, which offered inclusive holidays mainly to the Isle of Man. They paid a fixed rate for a vehicle enabling them to offer individual bookings on their holidays.

Ribble were also having discussions with the Pool regarding through running South of Cheltenham on hire to the Pool. Through coaches between Liverpool and Paignton and Bournemouth commenced in 1955 operating daily during the summer with additional vehicles on Friday and Saturday nights. Various changes were made over the years but the principal of through running remained. Black & White crews were involved with a changeover at Cheltenham.

In 1957 the Suez Crisis brought problems with a 50% cut in fuel to operators. Ribble operated to Cheltenham at weekends only while Yelloway also reduced operations accordingly. By Easter the situation had been resolved with the fuel rationing scheme ending. There were after-effects with the Pool withdrawing all night services from the coast on Friday nights to Cheltenham. This did not affect Yelloway departures, which continued operating the regular timetable but the withdrawal of the 2.30am on Sunday morning also meant the withdrawal of the Ribble Service from Liverpool on Saturday nights.

Royal Blue still operated the 8.00am from Exeter on Sunday mornings to Cornwall but with the withdrawal of the Pool connections to Exeter the departure was not served from the North-West. Yelloway came to an agreement with Royal Blue whereby passengers changed at Exeter instead of Cheltenham and was able to offer the full weekend facility again.

In 1964 Yelloway commenced a seasonal route to Torquay serving such places as Ashton under Lyne, Stockport, Macclesfield and Leek, joining the main route at Newcastle under Lyme.

The Yorkshire Battle 1952 - 1956

From 1947 passengers from Yorkshire had two routes to Cheltenham to connect with the Pool services. The first was by Yorkshire Services to Birmingham but passengers could not arrive in Cheltenham before 7.00pm, which left Weston super Mare and Cardiff as the only destinations available. The second route was by either Hebble or Hanson stage carriage service to Rochdale or Oldham to connect with the Yelloway services arriving in Cheltenham to serve the 2.00pm departures.

By 1952 Yorkshire Services had been licensed for an early morning timing to Birmingham with a connection by the Pool to Cheltenham arriving in time for the 4.00pm departures. West Yorkshire introduced a through vehicle to Bournemouth going on hire to the Pool south of Birmingham but there was still no connection for Torquay, which was a popular destination. Yelloway had expanded its timings to include a Saturday night service as well as Friday night returning on Friday and Saturday nights; this meant that Cornwall could be reached in one day.

Arrangements were made for both Hanson and Hebble to operate through coaches from Huddersfield, Bradford and Halifax not only to Torquay but also to Bournemouth and Southsea via Cheltenham and on hire to the Pool. By 1953 the Yorkshire independent operators were looking with some envy at the vast number of passengers who were going over the hill to Lancashire to commence their journeys to the South-West: traffic which they felt should have been carried by them.

J W Kitchin made the first application for a service between Bradford/Leeds and Torquay followed by O C Holdsworth on similar lines,

Underfloor-Engined Bristols

These Red and White vehicles represent the standard Bristol/Eastern Coach Works underfloor-engined designs to be found on Pool services in the nineteen-sixties. **UWO 705** (above) was a 1959 Bristol MW6G with a 39-seat coach body. It was photographed bound for London when brand new. In the picture below the later version of the MW6G, still a 39-seater, is seen on Red & White's 1962 delivery **109 CWO** in Pimlico Road, not far from Victoria Coach Station. (Both: Keith Healey Collection)

then a joint application from Wallace Arnold and Hansons for two services to Torquay from Leeds and Bradford. The four operators decided to show a united front and withdrew the applications, replacing them with a joint application with more picking up points and Huddersfield as the interchange point.

Further applications were lodged by Yorkshire Services for a Friday evening service between Bradford and Birmingham to connect with the Pool departure at midnight to Cheltenham for the 2.30am departures. All the applications were refused by the Traffic Commissioners whose decision was upheld on appeal to the Minister in 1955.

There was however a grant made in 1954 for the Fawdon Omnibus Company to operate a Friday night service between Newcastle on Tyne and Birmingham to connect with the 8.00am Pool service to Cheltenham. It picked up in Leeds at 2.50am plus other points in Yorkshire and served a very limited need.

In 1956 further applications were made by the independents for services to Torquay. This time the operators, including Hansons, Wallace Arnold and Kitchin, each applied for its own licence for the period of operation July and August only. Yorkshire Services also applied for a route direct to Torquay as well as a Bournemouth service but neither involved the Pool. Wallace Arnold also submitted a Bournemouth application.

Yelloway was very concerned about the abstraction of their Yorkshire traffic if any of the applications were granted and responded with a joint service with Hebble Motor Services from Bradford, Halifax, Huddersfield and Rochdale to Torquay. An example of traffic carried from Yorkshire can be seen from the previous year on Halifax Holidays. A total of 598 passengers were booked to travel on the Friday night, sixteen coaches were required, four each from Hebble and Yelloway, with another eight hired in by Yelloway. Eleven vehicles went to Torquay, the other five carrying Pool passengers to Bournemouth and Southsea. A further seven coaches were required to cater for the Saturday morning traffic. These were passengers that neither Yelloway nor the Pool could afford to lose.

By March 1956 Yelloway realised that bookings from Huddersfield were well down compared to previous years. Hanson refused to hire any vehicles to Yelloway and also refused to hire from Yelloway any vehicle to operate on their stage carriage service to Oldham and informed intending passengers that it was not possible to guarantee connecting facilities from Huddersfield to Oldham. They seemed very sure that a service would be granted them in time for the summer season.

The Minister when giving his decision on the 1954 applications put forward some interesting points to the statement made by the Chairman of the Yorkshire Traffic Commissioners. The Traffic Commissioner felt that where the same vehicle was intended to carry the same passengers on long journeys covered by more than one Road Service Licence of more than one operator, the licensing system was being evaded and he proposed the total prohibition of through running on such linked services. Fortunately the Minister did not agree with him as this would be against public interest but did consider that applications should disclose whether linking is proposed or not. However a further comment from the Minister was to cause problems in the future. He stated an operator was only entitled to consideration as an existing operator by reference to the service he runs not by reference to services on which his vehicles work under hire arrangements to another operator. This, of course, affected the Pool who had opposed all the applications except the one by Yorkshire Services on the grounds that they operated by linking at Birmingham suitable facilities to Torquay and other destinations.

On the first day of the 1956 hearing Counsel for Wallace Arnold questioned the right to appear in court (locus standi) of all the operators who were objecting and quoted the appeal decision of the previous applications that none of the operators had standing as objectors because they did not operate a similar service. Although this was heavily contested by the other Counsel, Major Eastwood, Chairman of the Traffic Commissioners, agreed and stated that representation could only be made by the objectors who then asked for an adjournment as they felt the ruling of no right of appeal might well have to be taken to the High Court

Yelloway in the Postwar Era

Above: **LDK 35**, *a Yelloway AEC Reliance with Burlingham Seagull coachwork, is seen at Cheltenham during its layover waiting to return to Rochdale at 4.30pm. Delivered in 1954, it was the third order for this combination and AEC became Yelloway's main chassis choice for the next 25 years. (Keith Healey Collection)*

Below: *The unusual bodywork on* **HDK 804**, *a Leyland Royal Tiger, is by Trans-United Coach Craft, a consortium of north-west coach operators led by Yelloway, who overcame the shortage of coach bodies after the war by building their own. This one dates from 1951 and was one of the last to be built for the Yelloway fleet. It was at Bristol on the direct Torquay service. (D Haddock Collection)*

as this could have far reaching implications in the licensing field. Although Wallace Arnold resisted the adjournment request Major Eastwood agreed. A few days later he reversed his decision and granted locus for them to pursue their objections. When the case was resumed Major Eastwood laid down a few ground rules. The case had not to be prolonged unnecessarily, he would stop cross examination if it appeared that the question was irrelevant, frivolous, vexatious or time-wasting and did not assist in ascertaining the facts. Also the case should be completed in the five days allocated. These remarks caused comments in the trade journals about the powers of the Traffic Commissioners to make such a ruling.

It was not until December that the Traffic Commissioners gave their decision. They granted a licence to Hanson restricted to Huddersfield engineering and textile holidays. Kitchin and Wallace Arnold were similarly restricted respectively to Bradford and Leeds holiday fortnight. All other applications were refused. This of course led to a further round of appeals which were heard in 1957. In May 1958 the Minister gave his decision dismissing all the appeals and it was a further seven years before any further applications were to be made.

Yorkshire and Joint Services 1965 - 1968

In June 1965 Crosville became a Pool member surrendering its part of the Bangor to Cheltenham licence. This left only one jointly operated service with Southdown Motor Services to Eastbourne. It had not been Pool policy to encourage joint operation but times were changing and thoughts were given to the Yorkshire - Torquay appeal decision given by the Minister some years ago about linked services and objections. This brought about a bigger involvement in joint operation in forthcoming years.

Nineteen-sixty-five will be long remembered for what became the most controversial application in the history of licensing. It began with the application for a service to Cheltenham and the South-West under the name of Yorkshire - Torbay Pool Partners of East Parade, Harrogate, this being

the Head Office of the West Yorkshire Road Car Co Ltd. Four routes were requested: Keighley - Cheltenham with feeder connections at Wakefield, from Halifax and Leeds, with an additional summer service to Torquay from Keighley again served by the two feeder routes. There were also linking conditions to operate through vehicles across Cheltenham and Exeter on services operated by either Associated Motorways or Royal Blue. A fortnight later an amendment appeared in Notices and Proceedings detailing the operators who formed the partnership. They were East Yorkshire, West Yorkshire, Yorkshire (WD), Yorkshire Traction and East Midland, who comprised the Yorkshire Services Pool, plus Yelloway, Hebble Motor Services, Wallace Arnold and J W Kitchin and the Pool. If granted, certain existing licences for services operated by Wallace Arnold, J W Kitchin and Hebble would be surrendered.

Objections were lodged by Hanson because of its Huddersfield - Torquay service and by Sheffield United Tours who had over the years built up, sometimes jointly with G C Littlewood, services to the South-West from Sheffield, Dronfield and Chesterfield. These points were included in the new application. British Rail, together with two coach operators of inclusive tours, objected as well.

On the first day of the hearing the application fell apart with the Counsel for the objectors submitting that the applicants did not constitute a legal partnership and this caused the application to be withdrawn.

In January 1966 another try was made with all the operators submitting separate applications for the four services with the condition that they were to be operated jointly with each other. This attracted nearly the same parade of objectors as had the previous application.

When the hearing was resumed the objectors raised points of law and applied to the High Court for an Order of Prohibition in an attempt to compel the Yorkshire Traffic Commissioners to disclose the financial particulars supplied to them by the applicants. Again the hearing was relisted, this time for six days commencing Wednesday, 9th November 1966, some seventeen months after the original application had been made.

Bristol Greyhound in the Postwar Era

Above: Bristol Greyhound No. **2821** *(**OHY 993**), a 1952 Bristol LWL6B with Eastern Coachworks 37-seat coachwork, is seen at Southsea after working in from Bristol. The vehicle was withdrawn in May 1965 and found its way into the fleet of McGregor, of Sible Hedingham. (Keith Healey Collection)*

Below: A more modern Bristol/ECW vehicle from the Greyhound fleet, No. **2112** *(**405 LHT**) was a 39-seater dating from 1961. With the full Bristol Greyhound fleetname, it was operating to Bristol with connections on to Cheltenham. This coach suffered serious damage in an accident in January 1970 and was scrapped the following April. (John Fozard Collection)*

The Traffic Commissioners granted licences for the summer period, not throughout the year as requested. Protection was given to Hanson, Sheffield United Tours and Littlewood on certain dates and timings to common destinations. The overall linking condition was cut to certain routes only and there were also duplication restrictions. In order to pacify centre holiday operators block bookings could not be made on the service on which inclusive holidays could be offered. Both Yorkshire Services and Yelloway were not allowed to advertise connecting facilities from Yorkshire via Birmingham or Rochdale as in the past. In fact Yorkshire Services lost the extra vehicle allowance to Birmingham they had been granted some years before to cater for the traffic, and the Fawdon service, now known as the Ten Cities Express, although not restricted, in their 1967 publicity showed the last picking up point on the Friday night service as Harrogate for connection with the Pool at Birmingham.

Because of the time taken to get the licence it was important that the public were made aware as soon as possible of the new facility. For the first time an advertisement was placed on television to promote just one route. Seven fifteen-second slots were broadcast on the Granada Yorkshire transmitter between 22nd March and 6th April for the "South West Clipper", as it was now called.

On the first departure in May 29 passengers were carried and over 5,000 advance bookings had been received. The largest mileage allocation in the Yorkshire - Torbay Pool of 28% was held by Yelloway.

At the other end of England in the South-East a similar exercise was being carried out. Travel House of Luton had operated a service from Stevenage to Cardiff for a few years but in 1965 three applications were made for new services. Firstly Grey Green Coaches between Felixstowe and Cheltenham, then Premier Travel for a Harwich - Clacton - Cheltenham service and finally the Pool also with a route between Felixstowe and Cheltenham. After discussions including Travel House a joint application was lodged by the four operators and on 1st July 1966 the "Eastlander" commenced linking Felixstowe, Harwich, Clacton on Sea via Ipswich to Cheltenham

with an additional 17 pickup points, nearly all new to the Pool.

Nineteen-sixty-six also saw a service to Butlins Holiday Camp at Barry Island. The Cleethorpes service was extended to Grimsby and the Bangor service had an extension to Holyhead.

The Pool was involved in something new, to replace a closed railway line, the old Somerset and Dorset, with a coach service. Commencing 7th March 1966 a twice-daily service was operated between Bristol and Bournemouth via Bath and Blandford.

The opening of the Severn Bridge on 8th September enabled the Pool to reduce the travelling time between London and South Wales by avoiding Cheltenham and established an interchange at the Austral Cafe, Caerwent, for other destinations in Wales not served by the direct route. They were also able to reduce fares from Wales to the south-west coast because of the saving in mileage. Connecting services from Caerwent to Bristol and Exeter gave such journeys as Neath to Weymouth a saving of four hours and 17/6d (88p) on the return fare.

Nineteen-sixty-seven saw the Pool being involved in further joint services. The Yorkshire - Torbay Pool had commenced but Yelloway was looking at revising its weekend services via Cheltenham and on 26th May commenced four new routes jointly with the Pool. Departing Lancashire Friday night and Saturday day, returning Saturday day and night they were to Minehead and Ilfracombe, Weymouth, Bournemouth finally Southampton and Portsmouth; with the last picking up point at Altrincham they then travelled direct to their destination. The following year a further joint service, this time on Saturday only, was commenced serving Monmouth, Newport, Cardiff and Barry Island.

Ribble in 1967 were also concerned with a joint service from Blackpool to Cheltenham and Paignton operating on the same days as the Yelloway/Pool services with its last picking up point at Leyland. Numbered X34 it was renumbered X44 in 1969.

Yelloway and Ribble were also extending their catchment area with a joint service from Colne to Paignton with the usual connecting

Pool Operations at Nottingham

Above: A Royal Blue 1961 Bristol MW6G with a 39-seat Eastern Coach Works body is seen in July 1965 operating a feeder from Nottingham to Northampton to connect with the direct service to Portsmouth and Bournemouth. (G H F Atkins)

Below: Not having the Bristol chassis available to them, Black & White's new vehicles in 1951 were Leyland Royal Tigers with Willowbrook 33-seat bodies, later reseated to 37. Twenty were delivered, and **KDF 982** is shown in June 1952 operating the old favourite route to Cheltenham. (G H F Atkins)

facilities at Cheltenham and Exeter. Prior to this passengers from East Lancashire had had to travel to Preston or Manchester to join services to the South-West.

Also over the years Lancashire United Transport of Atherton had been booking agents for Yelloway and thousands of passengers had travelled on local services to connect with Yelloway at Manchester. LUT made application for a Friday night and Saturday day service to Cheltenham picking up in their operating area for connections with the Pool services. In later years the LUT Traffic Manager admitted to the author that it had been a "tongue in cheek" application to stir Yelloway into serving their area. If that was the case it certainly worked, with a joint Yelloway and LUT service to Paignton offering all the connections with the Pool and Royal Blue; it commenced the following year, 1969.

The Final Years 1969 - 1975

Further joint services were commenced by the Pool in 1969, firstly with Northern General from Newcastle on Tyne to Torquay via Cheltenham. This was subject to a drawn-out appeal by British Rail which had still not been settled by the Minister at the end of 1974. Traffic had increased to such an extent during that period including a winter service that it is unlikely the appeal would have been successful.

The second route was more complicated, involving Grey Green Coaches, Yelloway and the Pool operating from Haslingden to Brighton, Newhaven and Eastbourne travelling through the Rossendale Valley, Manchester, Stockport, Macclesfield and the Potteries. The Grey Green involvement was because of the services operated from London on which Yelloway made through bookings and of course the Pool operated connecting facilities from Cheltenham to Brighton and Eastbourne.

Southern National ceased to be an operational company and a Pool member with all its vehicles and routes being transferred to its sister company Western National whilst Ribble introduced a new service X26 from Southport to Cheltenham on weekends only

and at last the Bristol - Liverpool - Blackpool linked services were licensed as a through service. Winter operation from Yorkshire to Cheltenham was granted and commenced on 1st October.

To encourage traffic the Pool's return tickets issued on the Cardiff - Blackpool service from Cardiff to Chester and Liverpool were interchangeable with the X71 Cardiff - Liverpool service operated jointly by Crosville and Western Welsh. Return tickets on both services were also available, subject to a surcharge, on British Rail between these points.

Because of complaints from passengers having to wait at Butlins, Barry Island, until 2.30pm for the joint service to Manchester the service was revised in 1970 to depart at 10.00am. This meant the Pool was involved in operating part of the service for the first time.

Another joint service, this time with the East Kent Road Car Co Ltd, was commenced between Cheltenham/Margate and Ramsgate. An unusual through-booking arrangement was introduced whereby the Standerwick Blackpool - Oxford service offered connections onwards to Portsmouth and Bournemouth. It reduced the travelling time between Blackpool and Bournemouth by three hours. In 1972 the X44 joint service was amended to operate daily between Blackpool and Cheltenham and the connecting facility at Oxford was withdrawn, there now being no saving in time.

The Cheltenham - Blackpool route again attracted a new service, this time the extension to Cheltenham of the former Owens and Burnham services between Worcester and Blackpool which had been combined into one route by Midland Red and became jointly operated with Ribble in 1971.

On 2nd July 1971 a direct service between Bradford and Bournemouth was introduced by the joint Yorkshire - Torbay Pool. There were also revisions to the Eastlander route with the destinations of Clacton on Sea and Harwich being withdrawn, now being replaced by a connecting link from Colchester by the Essex Coast Express service from London.

Although the Severn Bridge had opened in 1966 it was not until 1972 that the M4 motorway was extended over it with the

Black & White Guys and AECs

Above: *Black & White tried the Guy LUF chassis and this example, **NDG 175**, was at Huntingdon Street, Nottingham, in June 1954 soon after its entry into service. The 37-seat coachwork was by Duple. (G H F Atkins)*

Below: *Seen at Victoria Coach Station in September 1962 on the direct service to Gloucester is **4216 AD**, a 1960 AEC Reliance, again with Duple bodywork, this time seating 41. (G H F Atkins)*

interchange now being at Aust Motorport. Further reductions in journey times could be made and more direct services into the south-west of England from South Wales. A direct Birmingham - Bristol service via the M5 motorway was introduced and a further service from Cheltenham to North Wales commenced, this time to Pwllheli. The Cheltenham - Derby route was extended to Ilkeston and Heanor.

The previous year the Worcester - London South Midland service and the London - Southend on Sea service operated by Eastern National had both been downgraded to stage carriage operation. This enabled the Pool to introduce in 1972 a direct twice-daily Worcester - Oxford - London service and a daily Cheltenham - Southend on Sea service via London Victoria Coach Station. Southdown Motor Services became a full member of the Pool thus bringing the members up to ten.

Nineteen-seventy-three was the last summer of operation by the Management Committee for the Pool and the writing was on the wall with the timetable displaying the word National on the front cover then Associated Motorways; nowhere else in the timetable was there reference to National. The last application for a new service was made in September for a joint route between Glasgow and Paignton operated by Midland Red, North Western, Ribble, Western SMT, Yelloway and the Pool. This brought about an unusual situation of a member company of the Pool, Midland Red, holding a licence in its own right to operate jointly with the Pool on the same service.

From October 1st National Travel (NBC) Ltd, the renamed London Coastal Coaches, took over the planning and operation of express services, which were divided into five areas and the Winter Timetable now not only included the Pool services but all the routes operated by Greyhound and Royal Blue - well worth 5p.

One further application was made to the Traffic Commissioners in December, by Black & White Motorways for the first express service by the company in its own right for nearly 40 years and it would be nice to think that it would have been a Pool application under normal circumstances. It was a daily

service from Cheltenham to Paris, its timing gave connections to and from all the destinations serving Cheltenham. Europe here we come.

By the early part of 1974 all the five National Travel areas had been formed into companies with Black & White Motorways becoming National Travel (South West). Pooling arrangements were now finished and any jointly operated services with non-NBC operators had new agreements made between the appropriate company and National Travel.

Summer 1974 saw the commencement of the Glasgow - Paignton service, and also a faster service between Hull and Cheltenham. In West Wales new services were operated from Fishguard, Cardigan, Newcastle Emlyn, Aberystwyth and Lampeter to the interchange at Caerwent and included through-running such as Cardiff - Eastbourne, Pembroke Dock - Paignton and Aberystwyth - Bournemouth. Gradually nearly all the Pool licences were transferred to National Travel (South West) with the remainder being passed to other National Travel Companies.

In its last year of operation the Member Companies totalled ten and apart from routes operated solely by the Pool there were in addition joint services with 15 other companies. Through booking arrangements were available with a further 18 operators where the Pool tickets were accepted on their services and served over one thousand towns and villages.

Finally it is interesting to note that an overall structure for express services had been discussed before Donald Sinclair, General Manager of Midland Red, had referred to it in a paper presented to the Institute of Transport in 1948. However in 1960, A F R Carling who was a BET Director, set up a small working party consisting of R K Cope of Midland Red who was now Chairman of the Management Committee, G Duckworth of Southdown and F W J Robinson of London Coastal Coaches. Their brief was to consider any advantage in adopting a national coaching network name and the possibility that closer-knit control of operations converging on main centres might lead to improvements and economy of operations. It came to the conclusion that the public were inadequately informed of the

Black & White 36ft-long Coaches

Above: Another new chassis type for Black & White, in 1969, was the Daimler Roadliner. In looks and potential this was a handsome machine but, unfortunately, that potential was never realised and the Roadliner was troublesome. There is no denying, however, that Black & White's examples looked the part, as shown by SRP8-model (the Perkins-engined variant) **RDG 305G** at Oxford Road, Llandudno, in July 1970. It was waiting to return to Cheltenham. The vehicle was prematurely withdrawn in 1975 but went on to serve three subsequent owners: none for long. (G H F Atkins)

Below: In another Nottingham view, Black & White **AAD 243B**, a 1964 Leyland PSU3/3R Leopard with Plaxton 47-seat coachwork, demonstrates a livery variation carried prior to the National Bus Company's corporate all-over white. The coach was pictured in August 1972 before leaving Nottingham's Victoria bus station for Cheltenham. The words "Associated Motorways" in the destination screen had been replaced by a new logo. (G H F Atkins)

extent of coach travel and a common front approach would inspire public confidence thus avoiding the present confusion from the multiplicity of company names and publicity. There should be a common name to apply to selected services which would form an express network. They wished to avoid using terms like Coachways, Motorways, National, etc., and came up with "Network Services". All companies would use a badge on all relevant publicity, for example "this is a Network Service", and all companies' vehicles operating on the Network would carry a similar slogan and badge thus identifying them with the Network: shades of the prewar Yorkshire - Blackpool services. Lastly, a small representative committee would be formed from the principal participating companies to implement the report. Carling passed the working party's scheme to Horace Bottomley of Ribble for his comments.

The heading to his eight-page reply was "National Coachways". He felt, like Carling

and Sinclair, that the public would think of "Network Services" as something to do with television. He then went on to analyse every aspect of the report including asking 'what is an "Express Service"', stating that although Ribble operated to Glasgow and Edinburgh from Lancashire, the service carried local passengers in certain areas. His biggest objection was to the proposed committee and he for one would not like to tell another company what services or timings to operate when he had no knowledge of its area. Many of the observations made in his letter referred to the setting up of a separate organisation with vehicles to operate the services and the same problems that had to be overcome by National Travel some twelve years later were put forward.

It was agreed that to make the scheme work both the Tilling and Scottish Bus Groups must be involved; however, there is no indication that this took place and the idea seems to have been forgotten.

Below: These ingenious graphs of quantity and origin of passenger traffic into Cheltenham (left) and out (right) relate to the 2.00pm group of services on 9th August 1952. (Bus & Coach)

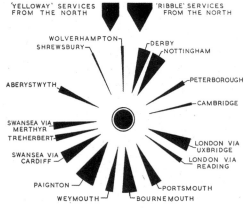

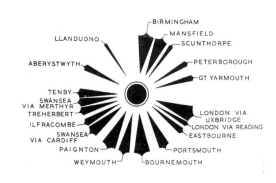

Tilling Group Bristols

Above: The opening of the M5 and M50 motorways enabled services from the Midlands to South Wales to bypass Cheltenham, resulting in a journey shortened by up to two hours. The first feeder was from Monmouth to Coventry, later extended through Leicester to Nottingham, where Red & White's 1966 Bristol RELH6G 47-seater **GWO 9D** was waiting to return to Monmouth in July 1971. The new logo is again in evidence, in the nearside destination screen. (G H F Atkins)

Below: The Lincolnshire Road Car Company's Bristol LS6G **MFU 106** demonstrates the unusual front-mounted route board for the "Express Coach Service between Scunthorpe and Cheltenham and the West". This vehicle was delivered new in March 1955, the service started in 1955, and it is believed that this type of route-detail presentation by LRCC occurred for a short period only at the commencement of the service. (R N Hannay)

The Final Years - 1

Above: *Even though the Pool finished in 1974, being subsumed into National Travel, certain independent operators continued to work jointly with the new organisation. New in 1978, Premier Travel* **RVE 296S**, *an AEC Reliance 6U32R type with Plaxton 49-seat body, worked on the "Eastlander" service until the coach station in Cheltenham closed in 1984. In this view it seems to be on a working not licensed to Premier Travel as it has an "On Hire to National Express" sticker in the windscreen. Premier Travel withdrew this AEC from service in 1990. (Keith Healey Collection)*

Below: *The last service to be licensed to the Pool was the direct Glasgow to Paignton in 1974. Yelloway* **HVU 247N**, *a 1975 AEC Reliance with Plaxton Panorama Elite III 49-seat body, is seen arriving at Cheltenham from the south. (Keith Healey Collection)*

The Final Years - 2

Above: In 1971 Black & White took delivery of **YDF 324K**, one of a batch of ten Leyland PSU3B/4R Leopards with Plaxton 47-seat coachwork. Seen in September 1972 at London Victoria on the direct Gloucester service, it was sporting the new National allover white livery with a very small "Black & White" fleetname above the front wheel arch. (G H F Atkins)

Below: Seen in its Cheltenham - Paris livery, **SND 296X**, a Leyland PSU5D/4R Leopard with Plaxton Supreme V 53-seat body, was delivered to National Travel (West) in 1981. The latter had, since August of that year, been responsible for the Cheltenham operations. (Keith Healey Collection)

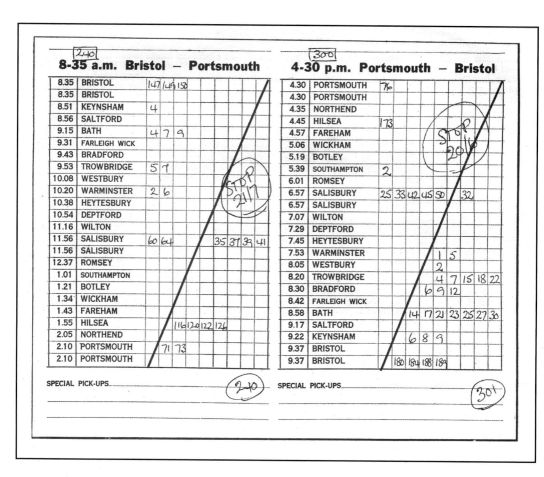

8-35 a.m. Bristol — Portsmouth		
8.35	BRISTOL	147 148 158
8.35	BRISTOL	
8.51	KEYNSHAM	4
8.56	SALTFORD	
9.15	BATH	4 7 9
9.31	FARLEIGH WICK	
9.43	BRADFORD	
9.53	TROWBRIDGE	5 7
10.08	WESTBURY	
10.20	WARMINSTER	2 6
10.38	HEYTESBURY	
10.54	DEPTFORD	
11.16	WILTON	
11.56	SALISBURY	60 64 35 37 39 41
11.56	SALISBURY	
12.37	ROMSEY	
1.01	SOUTHAMPTON	
1.21	BOTLEY	
1.34	WICKHAM	
1.43	FAREHAM	
1.55	HILSEA	116 120 122 126
2.05	NORTHEND	
2.10	PORTSMOUTH	71 73
2.10	PORTSMOUTH	

SPECIAL PICK-UPS _____ 2-10

4-30 p.m. Portsmouth — Bristol		
4.30	PORTSMOUTH	76
4.30	PORTSMOUTH	
4.35	NORTHEND	
4.45	HILSEA	173
4.57	FAREHAM	
5.06	WICKHAM	
5.19	BOTLEY	
5.39	SOUTHAMPTON	2
6.01	ROMSEY	
6.57	SALISBURY	25 33 42 45 50 32
6.57	SALISBURY	
7.07	WILTON	
7.29	DEPTFORD	
7.45	HEYTESBURY	
7.53	WARMINSTER	1 5
8.05	WESTBURY	2
8.20	TROWBRIDGE	4 7 15 18 22
8.30	BRADFORD	6 9 12
8.42	FARLEIGH WICK	
8.58	BATH	14 17 21 23 25 27 30
9.17	SALTFORD	
9.22	KEYNSHAM	6 8 9
9.37	BRISTOL	
9.37	BRISTOL	180 184 188 189

SPECIAL PICK-UPS _____ 301

Above: Inward and outward booking charts, in this case for an early 1950s Bristol to Portsmouth and return journey. Heavy demand had ensured that a stop had been put on bookings in both directions. These charts are further discussed on the opposite page. (Bus & Coach)

Below: Associated Motorways ticketing was a complicated business. Here are chart room and original copies for a journey from Swansea to London and return. (Bus & Coach)

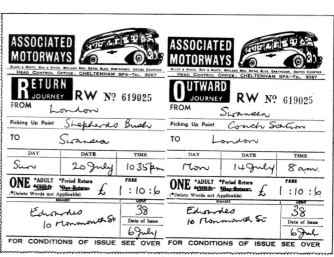

Through Ticketing

The Pool operation was mainly based on the interchange of passengers at Cheltenham, where all services connected at various times of the day. These services then made further connections with other Pool routes, so a full range of destinations could be reached. In the first Yorkshire application in 1954 when the operation of linked services with the running of through coaches over various licences was questioned, reference was made to an Appeal heard in 1932, known as the "Elliott Summation of Fares Appeal". Elliott Bros had applied to the West Midland Traffic Commissioners for various licences from Derby/Nottingham/Birmingham to Plymouth/Southsea/Bournemouth. The Elliott form of operation was quite simple: take three routes as an example, say A - B, C - D and E - F. By interchanging at given points passengers could travel from A - D or C - E or even F - A. One through ticket was issued and if required through coaches would be operated to avoid changing. Although this type of interchanging of passengers was done by Red & White as well as Black & White theirs was at one central point where in fact the services terminated. In Elliott's case transfers took place not only at X but at Y and Z as well, the services did not terminate at these points but carried on. In order to cover all the interchanging destinations, each licence applied for in the West Midland Traffic Area had an extra fare list showing fares to all the points reached by changing. The Chairman of the West Midland Traffic Commissioners granted the three routes applied for, but struck out the fare tables for through fares over connecting services, also refusing the operation of through vehicles over more than one route and no through tickets could be issued. It left Elliotts no alternative but to lodge an Appeal against the decision. The through ticketing over connecting services was also a bone of contention in other Traffic Areas. Yorkshire were refusing the Limited Stop Pool and the North Western were doing the same with Ribble, both concerns having to lodge Appeals.

The result of the Elliott Appeal overturned the West Midland Chairman's ruling, stating (1) the summation of fares was permissible on connecting services; if the through fare was to be less then the summation of the two fares on the two linked journeys, the appropriate fare should be shown on the licences; (2) the issue of through tickets was permissible; and (3) the linking of services by through vehicles was also permissible.

When the Pool was formed in 1934 this Appeal decision became the backbone of their operation. Fare tables were presented to the Traffic Commissioners showing summation fares for through bookings. This enabled one ticket with one fare to be issued for the journey even though a change of vehicle may be necessary en route. During the 1950s and 60s new Traffic Commissioners questioned this method of operation, especially in the West Midland Area, but the Appeal stood the test of time. In the case heard in Yorkshire in 1954 it was ruled that the Appeal only applied where all the licences were held by one company and not a link-up of various operators.

One example of how through running originates can be seen in the Booking Chart for the 8.35am from Bristol to Portsmouth. To the left of the thick line dividing the chart are the passengers boarding and on the right passengers alighting. This service also connects with the 7.30am Cheltenham to Bournemouth service at Salisbury. There are 64 passengers joining at that point and 41 alighting; so were these passengers to and from other destinations, is a through vehicle needed from Bristol to Bournemouth, or is one required from Cheltenham to Portsmouth? Looking also at the number alighting at Hilsea where connections can be made to resorts on the South Coast as far as Eastbourne, again: are there through bookings, does it require through coaches across Hilsea? By the time the final details of vehicle operations had been worked out by Cheltenham, all these questions would have been answered and inspectors at various points would know what through vehicles would be operated on the day.

1932 Summer Season   *As from March 21st*

THE SYMBOL OF SAFETY.

Royal Blue Automobile Services

Messrs. ELLIOTT BROS. (Bournemouth) LTD.

ROUTE J.   **Daily Services Between**   **TABLE 19.**

BOURNEMOUTH - GLOUCESTER
AND
COVENTRY

With Connections to and from BIRMINGHAM and the WEST OF ENGLAND

Interior photograph of one of our Regular Service Coaches. All our vehicles are of the very latest type 6-cylinder Daimler, A.E.C. Reliance, Regal Maudslay or Leyland Model Saloons or Sun Saloons. They are fitted with vacuum Servo four-wheel brakes, arm-chair seats, reading tables, travelling rugs, luggage accommodation, and all the latest improvements for the safety and comfort of passengers.

REGISTERED OFFICES :

68/70, HOLDENHURST RD., BOURNEMOUTH
'PHONE : 6262 (SIX LINES)

5,000 29/7/32

Left: Elliott Bros were very proud of their Duple-bodied coaches, of which both interior and exterior were shown on their timetable covers, as in this 1932 example. *Above:* The first edition of the short-lived publication *"By Coach"* had this advertisement for Pool services from London. *(Both: Keith Healey Collection)*

MIDLAND "RED"

AND RAILWAYS JOINT MOTOR SERVICES

SERVICE R

BIRMINGHAM & PAIGNTON

Via BRISTOL, EXETER, TEIGNMOUTH & TORQUAY

(Joint Service with Greyhound Motors Limited)

Time Table operative from SEPTEMBER 28th, 1931, until WHITSUNTIDE, 1932 (except December 25th).

Left: Midland Red express service leaflets were well known for their sketches of interesting places to be seen from coaches on such journeys, exemplified by this 1931 winter timetable for the Paignton service. (Keith Healey Collection)

Right and below: Fragments from a 1932/3 Black & White leaflet for services from Birmingham. This battered but complete document was discovered some 25 years later by the author behind a drawer in Manchester's Lower Mosley Street bus station. (Keith Healey Collection)

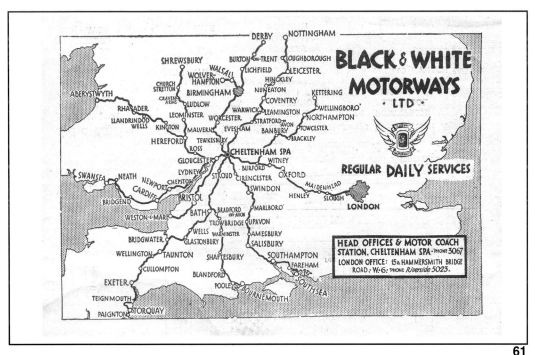

YELLOWAY MOTOR SERVICES LTD.

Reg. Office: WEIR STREET, ROCHDALE.   Tel. 3101-3102

DEVONIAN SERVICE
LANCASHIRE and TORQUAY
Via NEWCASTLE-U-LYME, STAFFORD, GLOUCESTER, BRISTOL, etc.

Operates SOUTH : Sunday, Wednesday, Friday, Saturday.

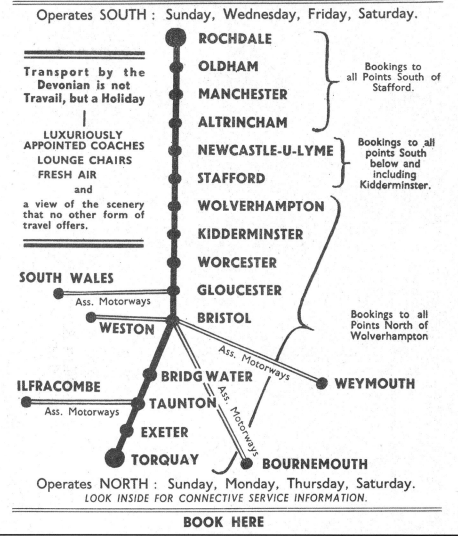

Transport by the Devonian is not Travail, but a Holiday

LUXURIOUSLY APPOINTED COACHES LOUNGE CHAIRS FRESH AIR and a view of the scenery that no other form of travel offers.

ROCHDALE
OLDHAM
MANCHESTER
ALTRINCHAM

Bookings to all Points South of Stafford.

NEWCASTLE-U-LYME
STAFFORD

Bookings to all points South below and including Kidderminster.

WOLVERHAMPTON
KIDDERMINSTER
WORCESTER
GLOUCESTER
SOUTH WALES
BRISTOL
WESTON
Ass. Motorways

Bookings to all Points North of Wolverhampton

BRIDGWATER
ILFRACOMBE
TAUNTON
Ass. Motorways
EXETER
TORQUAY
BOURNEMOUTH
WEYMOUTH
Ass. Motorways

Operates NORTH : Sunday, Monday, Thursday, Saturday.
LOOK INSIDE FOR CONNECTIVE SERVICE INFORMATION.

BOOK HERE

Above and right: Both Yelloway and Ribble included route maps on the front of their leaflets. The Yelloway example dates from 1935, just prior to their move into Cheltenham. Ribble's "Westlinks" had, by 1954 in its third season, been extended beyond Glasgow and Edinburgh to Thurso and Scrabster, which would have been useful for holidaymakers bound for Orkney and Shetland. (Both: Keith Healey Collection)

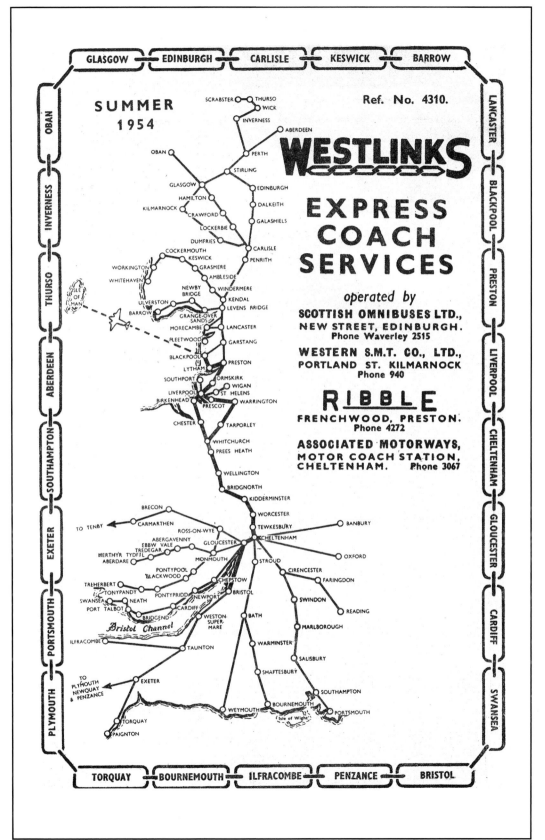

NATIONAL

ASSOCIATED MOTORWAYS

*EXPRESS
COACH
SERVICES*

LONDON

TO

WALES

AND

SOUTH MIDLANDS

SUMMER – 1973
MAY 20th to Sept. 29th

ASSOCIATED MOTORWAYS
COACH STATION - CHELTENHAM SPA - Telephone 26411

This Summer 1973 National leaflet was one of a series that were the last ever produced bearing the title "Associated Motorways". (Keith Healey Collection)